DESIGN and MAKE

Simple Machines

Fran Whittle
Sarah Lawrence

WAYLAND

DESIGN and MAKE

Houses and Homes
Things to Wear
Toys and Games
Water Projects
Wheels and Transport

First published in 1997 by Wayland Publishers Ltd,
61 Western Road, Hove, East Sussex BN3 1JD, England
© Copyright 1997 Wayland Publishers Ltd
Series planned and produced by Margot Richardson
Find Wayland on the internet at http://www.wayland.co.uk

British Library Cataloguing in Publication Data
Whittle, Fran
Simple Machines. – (Design & Make)
1.Machinery – Juvenile literature
2.Handicraft – Juvenile literature
I.Title   II.Lawrence, Sarah
745.5

ISBN 0 7502 2101 1

Commissioned photography by Zul Mukhida
Cover photography by APM Studios
Designed by Tim Mayer
Edited by Margot Richardson
Equipment supplied by Technology Teaching Systems Ltd, Alfreton, UK
Printed and bound in Italy by G. Canale & C.S.p.A., Turin

CONTENTS

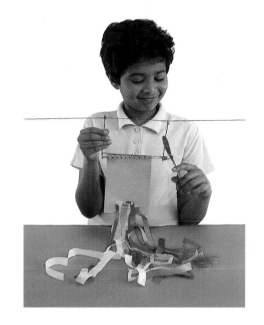

INTRODUCTION

Machines must have some energy put into them to make them work. The simplest machines use human or animal energy, but others use water, wind, tension, gravity, electricity, oil and gas.

Many mechanisms are very simple. More complicated ones are often made up of a lot of simple parts. Some mechanisms can do several jobs at once, work at different speeds and are made from many materials.

Throughout history, people have made machines because they wanted to do things which needed extra strength or speed, such as ploughing a field, or travelling in a cart pulled by a horse. Machines can also do work which needs actions to be done over and over again: for example, putting food into packets.

Machines are getting more complicated all the time, and some have computers built into them. This machine is a type of robot. It is building cars.

Musical instruments have mechanisms that are worked by people to make sounds. Bagpipes have air blown into them. The air is then pumped out by squeezing the bag.

Making good machines came through trial and error, sometimes accidentally, and by knowing how the human body worked.

A machine needs to be right for the job to be carried out. The design must use materials that are strong enough, and must think about the environmental effects, such as fumes made by petrol engines.

Many toys have moving parts. These toys are all more than 100 years old. Some are just pushed along. Others are wound up with a key, like an old clock.

WAVING ARMS

YOU WILL NEED

- Cardboard box, about 25cm square
- Three strips of thick cardboard, about 6cm wide and 35cm long
- Thin cardboard for face and hands
- Large metal paper fastener
- Hole punch
- Glue stick
- Pencil
- Ruler
- Scissors
- Paint and paintbrushes

This is a machine that uses levers. It has three levers that are all joined together. Pull and push one lever to make the others work in different directions.

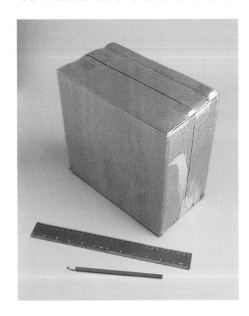

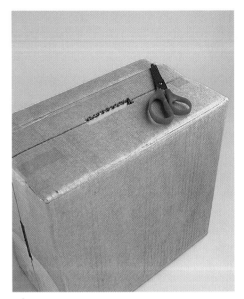

1 Using the pencil and ruler, measure the centre line of the box, up both sides and over the top.

2 In the centre of each line, mark a slot just big enough to take the card strips. Each slot should be about 6.5cm long and 1cm wide.

A see-saw is a very large lever with the pivot in the middle. Pushing down on one end makes the other end rise up. This simple mechanism has been used for different machines since ancient times.

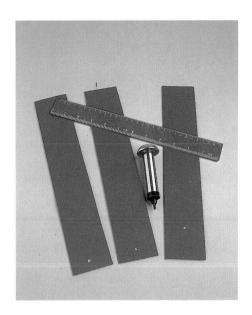

3 Make small holes in the ends of the card strips. On two strips the holes should be about 2cm from one end. On the other strip, the hole should be about 5cm from the end.

4 Draw a face and hands on the thin cardboard. Cut them out, and paint them. Also decorate the box.

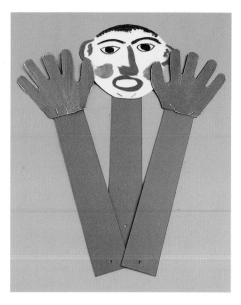

5 Glue the hands to the two shorter strips of card, at the opposite ends to the holes. Glue the face to the longer strip.

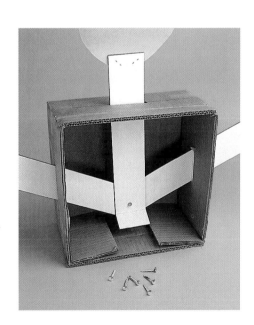

6 Bend the longer strip about 3cm from the end with the hole. Slide the ends of the strips into the slots in the box. Fasten them together loosely with the paper fastener.

7 Pulling a side strip in and out will make the top strip wave to and fro. Pushing the bent handle of the long strip up and down will make the side strips wave up and down.

MYSTERIOUS ROLLERS

Impress your friends with a mystery machine that has been a toy for many years.

YOU WILL NEED

- Tall cardboard box
- Two wide card tubes at least 10cm longer than the width of the box
- Used gift-wrapping paper
- Sticky tape
- Glue stick
- Pencil
- Ruler
- Scissors
- Paint and paintbrushes (optional)

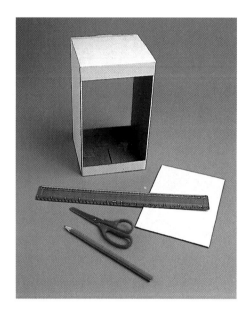

1 If the box has flaps, close them and tape them shut. On two opposite sides of the box, mark with a pencil and then cut out most of the sides. Leave some cardboard behind at the top and the bottom, to make the box stronger.

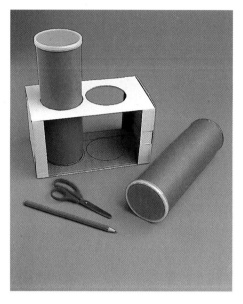

2 On one side of the box, put the end of the tubes about 1cm apart. Draw round them and cut out the holes. Push the tubes through and draw round them on the other side. Cut out the circles. Push the tubes through the box.

Rollers are used in many different machines. These women in Bangladesh are using rollers to make paper.

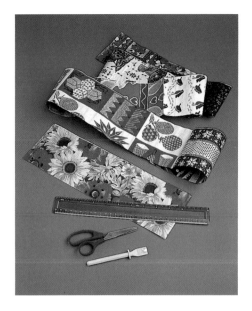

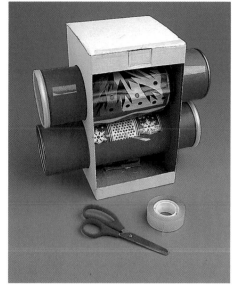

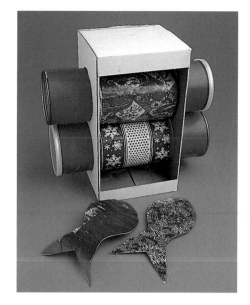

3 Cut the wrapping paper into strips wide enough to fit on the rollers inside the box. Glue them together to make a piece about 1.5 metres long that is patterned on both sides.

4 Tape one end of the paper strip to the top roller, and wind all the paper on to it tightly. Thread the other end between the rollers and tape the end to the lower roller on the other side, so it makes an 'S' shape from the side. Wind a little paper back on to the lower roller.

5 Draw and cut out one shape in two different colours. Wind one shape into the rolled paper. Keep turning, then turn the other roller and wind the second shape into the paper on the other side. It will seem to disappear, and as you keep winding, the first shape will appear again.

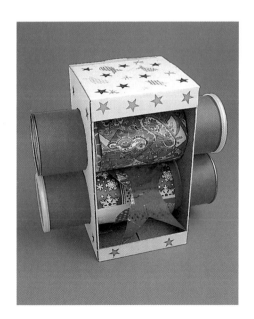

6 Decorate the box to match the paper. It helps if you mark or decorate the box to remember which side is which.

NOW TRY THIS

Make some shapes that look as if they change into each other in the rollers: for example, a cat into a dog, a superhero into a mouse, or a tadpole into a frog.

FLYING MESSENGER

The energy stored in a twisted rubber band can turn a propeller. You can fly the messenger along a line stretched between two walls, or two pieces of furniture. Attach a message to surprise your friends or family.

You will need to ask an adult to help you bend the wire.

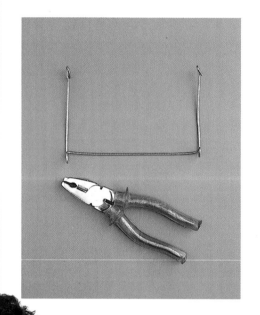

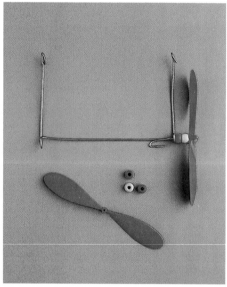

1 Bend the wire as shown in the photograph. Each side should be about 15cm long. Make a closed loop at each end of the wire.

2 Open the paper clip leaving a hook at one end. Put the propeller on it, then the beads. Thread the straight end of the paper clip through a wire loop and make it into a hook again.

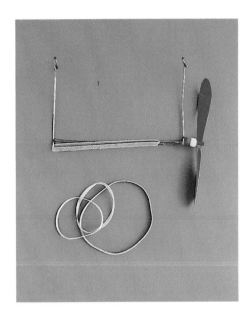 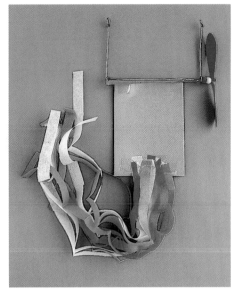 

3 Put the rubber band on the other wire loop and stretch it so that it goes over the hook of the paper clip. Make sure the band is stretched so that it stays on.

4 Write a message on the card. Decorate the lower edge with streamers made from coloured paper. Stick the top of the card to the wire frame with sticky tape.

5 Thread the line through the top loops of the flyer. Tie the line in position. Put your machine in the middle of the line. Wind up the propeller at least 50 times and let go.

NOW TRY THIS

Fly a message to a friend next door. Change the size of the wire frame and the propeller and see what happens.

Old clocks get their energy from springs made of metal. The springs are wound up until they are tight. As they unwind they let go of energy in the same way as the wound-up rubber band that is used on this page.

11

WEIGH-YOUR- SAVINGS BANK

Make a money bank that uses gravity to show how much you have saved. The more money you add, the further the pointer will go down the box.

YOU WILL NEED

- Cardboard box with lid, such as a shoe box
- Medium sized paper clip
- Small plastic tub
- Thin wire
- Two small rubber bands
- Thin card
- Sticky tape
- Stapler
- Pencil
- Ruler
- Scissors
- Felt-tip pens

1 In one end of the box, make two holes in the centre. Cut a slot for coins between the two holes and the bottom edge of the box. Make sure this slot is also in the centre.

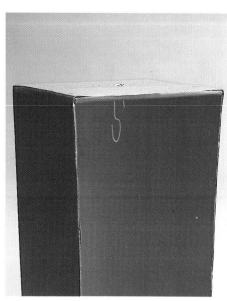

2 Unbend a paper clip and hook one end through the two holes. Let the other end hang down into the box.

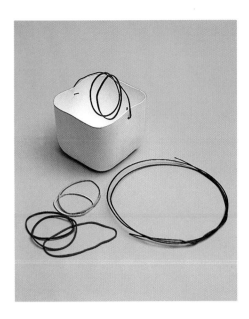

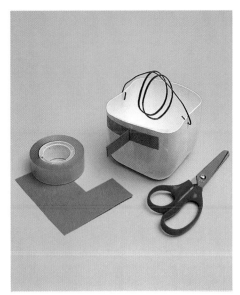

3 Make two small holes on either side of the plastic tub. Make a wire handle. Put the two rubber bands on the handle.

4 Cut two pieces of card about 5 x 1cm. Staple them together in the middle. Open out the ends on one side. Use sticky tape to stick them firmly to the side of the tub.

Weighing is one way of working out how much there is of something. Food is often weighed so that people know how much to pay for it. This man is weighing and selling bananas in Greece.

5 Cut a slit down the centre of the bottom of the box. It should be about 5mm wide. Start it about 8cm from one end of the box. Hang the tub on the hook of the paper clip.

6 Poke the card stuck to the tub through the slit. Make a card arrow and stick it to the card poking through the slit. Draw the weighing scale next to the slit. Put the lid on the box and hold it on with rubber bands. Now start saving.

NOW TRY THIS

Design and make a portion-weighing machine for food. It could be for something such as rice, breakfast cereal – or even dry pet food.

13

DRUM MACHINE

This machine makes a steady rhythm. Winding the handle changes the movement from round and round to up and down. This is the same mechanism as the one used in sewing machines.

This Chinese woman is using a sewing machine that is driven by her feet. The wheel near her feet is joined with a drive belt to the wheel on the machine. The machine changes the movement of the wheel to a movement that makes a sewing needle go up and down.

YOU WILL NEED

- Medium sized cardboard carton, approx 25 x 15 x 15cm
- Two strips of stiff cardboard, about 7.5cm wide and 45cm long
- Piece of straight, stiff wire, about 30cm longer than the cardboard carton
- Two large paper clips
- Four cotton reels
- String or thick thread
- Large rubber band
- Masking or sticky tape
- Pliers
- Scissors

1 Make a small hole in one strip of card, about 2.5cm from the end. Cut a slot in the end of the other piece, about 2.5cm long.

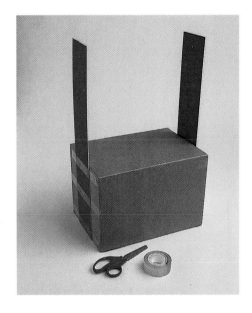

2 Turn the box so that a smooth side faces upwards. Stick the strips to the sides of the box with masking or sticky tape.

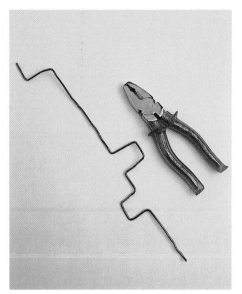

3 Bend the wire into the shape shown in the photograph. The shapes in the middle are called cranks. They must fit between the two cardboard strips. The piece of wire is called a crankshaft.

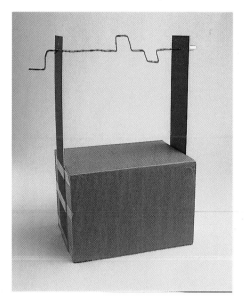

4 Put the end of the crankshaft into the hole and the handle end into the slot. Put a rubber band over the slot to hold the crankshaft down. Wind tape around the shaft's end to hold it in place.

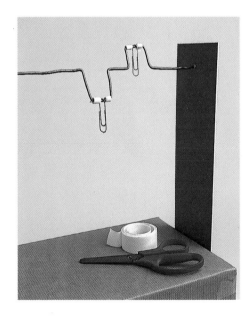

5 Put paper clips on to the bends in the crankshaft and wrap tape on both sides of each crank to keep the paper clips loosely in place.

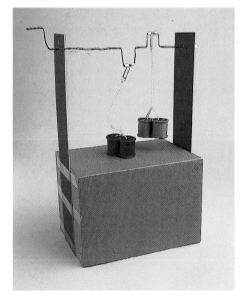

6 Tie two cotton reels on to a piece of string. Tie the other end to a paper clip. Turn the handle to check that the reels strike the box, and change the length of the thread if necessary. Repeat with the other cotton reels and paper clip.

NOW TRY THIS

● Try out different strikers and surfaces, such as upside-down yogurt pots striking a baking tray, or wooden beads striking wood.

● Make a machine with a larger box and a longer crankshaft with more cranks and strikers.

MOUSE-A-PULT

Here is a machine that lets you play a fun game with a cat. The mouse is catapulted away from the box. You can then 'rescue' the mouse by winding it back into its hole.

YOU WILL NEED

- Medium sized box, made from stiff cardboard, approx 20 x 20 x 10cm

- Thin plastic ruler, approx 30cm long

- Two pieces of wooden dowel, approx 5mm diameter and about 10cm longer than the width of the box

- Cardboard tube, about 4cm diameter

- Three large rubber bands

- Small 'mouse' made from paper, fabric or an old sock

- 1.5m thin cord or string

- PVA glue

- Hole punch

- Hand drill and drill bit

- Scissors

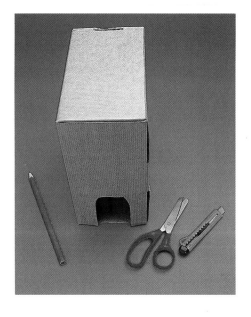

1 Cut a mouse hole in the box. It is easiest to do this on the bottom of the side that opens. Cut a slot for the ruler on the corner diagonally opposite the mouse hole.

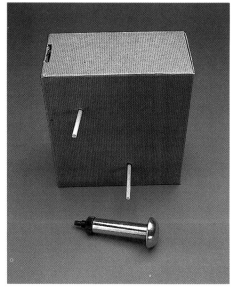

2 Punch holes in the sides of the box for the two dowels. Make sure the holes are opposite each other. Push the dowels through.

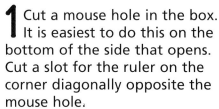

Catapults were used in fighting by the ancient Greeks, Romans, and in the Middle Ages. See the catapult throwing rocks in the bottom right corner of this old painting.

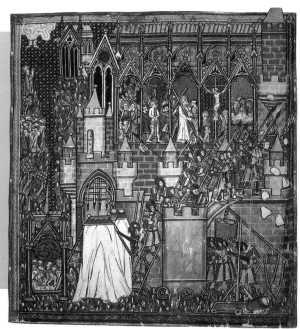

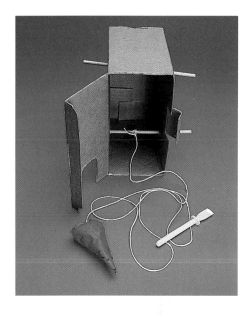
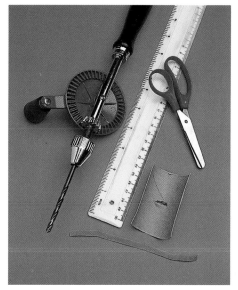
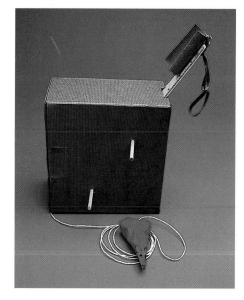

3 Tie one end of the string on to the mouse. Tie the other end to the middle of the dowel near the mouse hole. Add a little glue to hold the string on the dowel.

4 Ask an adult to help you drill a small hole in the ruler, about 2.5cm from one end. Cut some cardboard tube to form a cradle for the mouse. Tie the cradle on to the ruler, through the hole, with a rubber band.

5 Put the other end of the ruler into the slot on the top of the box. Make sure it goes down behind the two dowels. Tie on two more rubber bands at the top.

6 Put the mouse-a-pult at least 2 metres away from the cat. Put the mouse in the cradle. Make sure the string is hanging clear of the dowels. Put one hand on the box to hold it and pull down on the rubber bands. Let go and fire the mouse towards the cat. Slowly or quickly turn the bottom dowel until the mouse disappears into the hole, chased by the cat.

NOW TRY THIS

What is the longest piece of string you can catapult out. Does the weight of the mouse make any difference?

MINI SPREADER

YOU WILL NEED

- Corrugated plastic (or card)
- Lid of a plastic 35mm film canister
- Medium sized paper clip
- Old plastic pen top (or 2cm length of PVC tube)
- Three small metal paper fasteners
- Small foil pie dish or plastic lid, approx 8–10cm diameter
- Masking tape
- Pliers
- Bradawl
- Pencil
- Ruler
- Scissors

Take care when using a bradawl to make holes.

- **Hold the object in a vice if possible.**
- **Ask an adult to show you what to do.**

Use this mini machine for spreading sugar on your breakfast cereal or sugar strands on a slice of bread and butter.

You may need to ask an adult to help you make holes in parts of this machine. Start with really small holes: you can always make the holes larger, but not smaller.

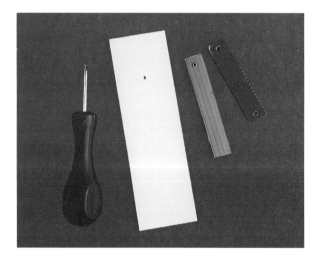

1 Cut a piece of corrugated plastic about 20 x 5cm. Make a hole about 4cm from one end. Cut another piece about 8 x 1cm, and make a small hole in one end. Cut a third piece about 6 x 1cm and make small holes in both ends.

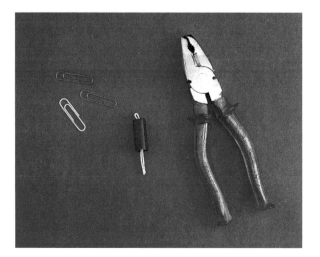

2 Using the pliers, open out the paper clip, then bend it in half. Make a hole in the top of the pen top with the bradawl, and push the ends of the wire through, leaving a little loop sticking out at the top.

Wipers on windscreens work in the same way as the Mini Spreader. The wipers are kept in check so that they just cover the windscreen, rather than going right round in a circle.

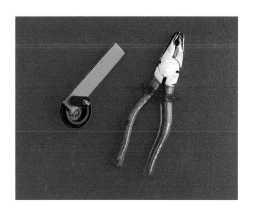

3 Turn the plastic film lid so that it is upside down with the lowest part in the centre. Make a hole in the side. Push the paper clip ends through the hole in the longer plastic strip, then through the side of the lid. Open them out in the groove underneath.

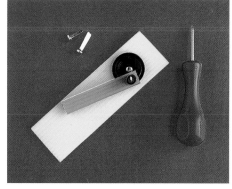

4 Make a hole in the centre of the plastic lid. Join it to the large piece of corrugated plastic with a paper fastener.

5 At the end of the corrugated plastic, make a bridge over the plastic strip with the other small piece of plastic, and fasten it to the base with two small paper fasteners.

6 Make many small holes in the base of the dish. Cut a slot half-way down the side of the dish and push the plastic strip though it. Stick it on underneath with masking tape.

7 Turn the pen-top handle in a circle to spread sugar on your cereal.

19

BUBBLE MACHINE

YOU WILL NEED

- Two rectangular plastic food tubs
- Two or three other plastic tubs and lids
- Medium-thickness wire, long enough to go through all the parts of the machine, plus about 10cm
- Three plastic film canisters with snap-on lids
- Seven plastic beads that will fit on the wire
- Plastic parcel tape
- Pliers
- Bradawl
- Scissors
- Marker pen that will draw on plastic
- Ruler
- Bubble mixture

Take care when using a bradawl to make holes. See page 18.

This machine can work in two ways. Turn the handle and make bubbles by blowing, or put the machine outdoors on a windy day. If you are using it outdoors you will need to put something heavy in the bottom tub and fix its lid on tightly.

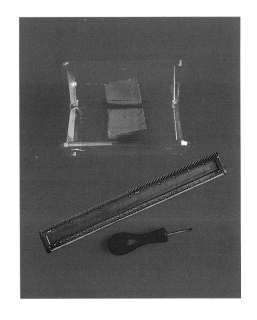

1 Measure the centre of the long sides of one tub. Using the bradawl, make a small hole on either side. Put the other tub underneath, upside down, and use parcel tape to join them together.

Wind was used to drive machines before electricity. These Dutch windmills had sails to catch the wind. Inside the windmill was machinery for grinding grain into flour, or pumping water out of low land.

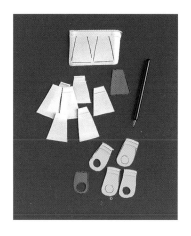

2 Using the templates, mark out eight wind vanes and four bubble paddles. Draw them on the edges of the spare plastic tubs and lids. Keep the narrow ends on the rims. Cut them out.

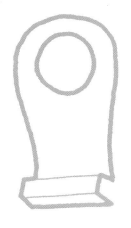

3 Carefully make a very small hole in the centre of the lids and bases of the film canisters. They must fit very tightly on the wire.

4 On each film canister, cut four evenly spaced slits down the sides. They should go three-quarters of the way down. Slide the rim ends of the vanes into the slits, and put the lids on the canisters.

5 Cut a piece of wire long enough to go through all the pieces, plus about 5cm. Make a small loop on one end of the wire.

6 Thread the other end through a bead, a film canister, two beads, the tub, a film canister, the other side of the tub, two beads, another film canister, and two more beads. Bend the end of the wire into a handle.

7 Fill the top tub with bubble mixture and you are ready to go.

NOW TRY THIS

Design different shapes and sizes of wind vane and bubble paddle. Do different shapes work better? What happens if you make the vanes and the paddles bigger?

COOKIE CRUSHER

YOU WILL NEED

- Medium sized cardboard carton with top opening, approx 20 x 15 x 25cm
- Stiff wire
- Flat plastic or foil food tray
- Empty food carton, filled with pebbles or sand
- Five pieces of wooden dowel, approx 5cm longer than the width of the box
- Five cotton reels
- Non-stretch cord
- Masking tape
- Pliers
- Scissors
- Pencil
- Ruler
- Cookies or crackers

You never know when you might need to share a cookie with a friend or make some crumbs to feed the birds. Pulley power lifts a heavy weight to break a cookie or cracker.

In these photographs the back of the box has been opened so you can see what is inside. There is no need for you to do this, however, when you make the Crusher.

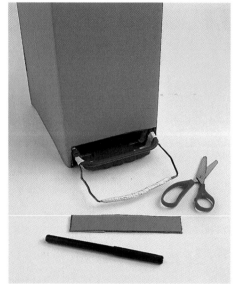

1 Bend a loop in the middle of the wire and bend the rest to go round the tray and make a handle. Use masking tape to join the wire to the sides of the tray. Wind masking tape around the handle.

2 Mark a hole in a short side of the box, big enough for the tray to slide in and out. Cut it out.

This Russian digger uses pulleys joined up with cables to lift its heavy scoop filled with earth.

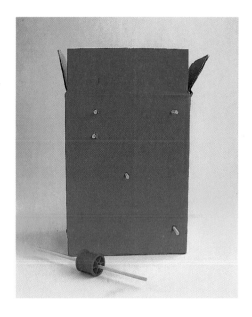

3 Make holes in the large sides of the box for the five dowel axles, in the places shown in the photograph. Push each dowel through one side of the box, through a cotton reel, and through the other side of the box.

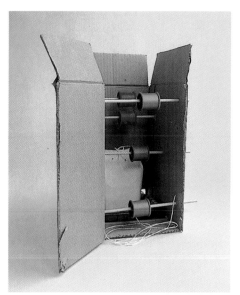

4 Tie one end of the cord securely to the wire loop on the tray. Slide the tray into the box so the front edge is level with the side of the box. Put the heavy carton in the tray.

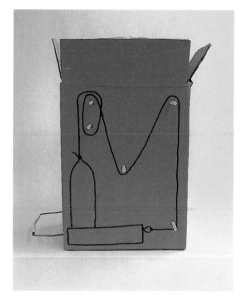

5 Put the string around the pulleys as shown on the box, in the photograph. Pull the string tight and mark where it gets to the top of the carton.

6 Take out the two axles above the carton. Tie the string to the carton so that the mark is exactly at the top of the carton. Put the carton, axles and pulleys back with the cord wound round them. Wind masking tape round the ends of the axles to keep them in place.

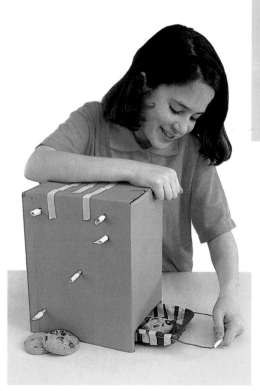

NOW TRY THIS

Try to make a printing machine. Put a piece of paper in the tray and stick a rubber stamp underneath the carton.

7 Hold the whole box steady and pull out the tray. Put a cookie in the tray and let go of it quickly. The heavy carton drops down and breaks the cookie.

TWIRLER

Cogs are used in many different places. This machine is being used to crush sugar cane to get out its sweet juice.

YOU WILL NEED

- Cardboard box with lid, such as a shoe box
- Wooden dowel, 5mm diameter, approx 6cm longer than the width of the box
- Small piece of wooden dowel, 5mm diameter, approx 3cm long
- Seven discs cut from corrugated card, approx 8cm diameter
- Matchsticks or cocktail sticks, cut to approx 2.5cm long
- PVA glue
- Sticky tape
- Hole punch
- Pliers
- Bradawl
- Ruler
- Scissors

Take care when using a bradawl to make holes. See page 18.

Cogs change a movement from one direction to another. Once you have made this machine, you can design a shape to fasten to the twirling wire. This could be a dancer or an ice skater, a model of an atom or the moon going round the earth.

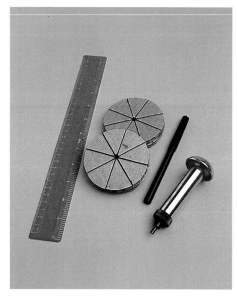

1 Take one card disc. Make two 4mm holes: one in the centre and another near the edge. Glue the small piece of dowel in the outer hole, then glue the disc on one end of the long dowel.

2 Glue the other card discs together in two lots of four. Let the glue dry. Make a 4mm hole in the centre of one thick disc. Mark out the top of both discs into eight equal parts.

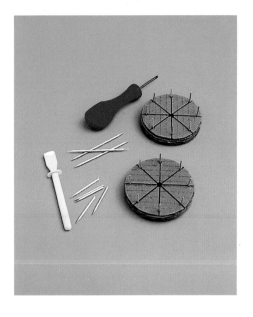

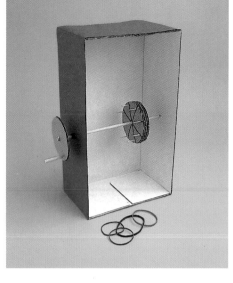

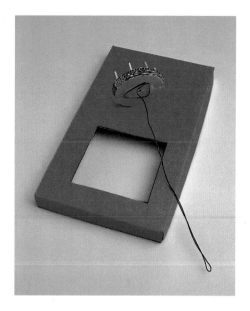

3 On each disc, use the bradawl to make eight holes on the lines, about 5mm in from the edge. Glue in the sticks and let the glue dry. The discs make two cogs.

4 Make a hole in the same place on each side of the box, about 5cm down from the top edge. Wind a rubber band round the dowel near the handle end, push it through one hole, through the cog and out through the other side. Wind a rubber band round the end of the dowel.

5 Bend one end of the thin wire into a triangle base. Tape it to the back of the other cog. Cut a hole in one end of the box lid so you can see what is going on underneath.

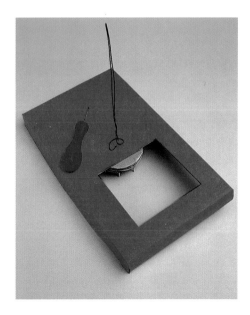

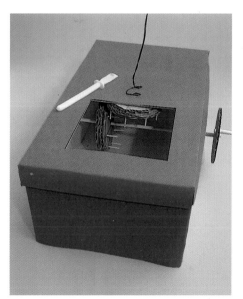

NOW TRY THIS
Try making the sizes of the cogs different. You could also change the numbers and the lengths of teeth on the cogs to see what happens.

6 Make a small hole in the centre of the lid, thread the wire through and bend it into a flat shape to hold the cog in place underneath.

7 Slide the cog on the dowel away from the centre so that the teeth of the two cogs meet when the handle is turned. Put a little glue round the hole and the dowel and let it dry.

25

BELLOWS

Bellows are used to push air. They are used to make a fire burn better by blowing air on to the burning wood or coal. Old pipe organs in churches used to have bellows to make their sound.

YOU WILL NEED

- Shoe box with well-fitting lid
- Large plastic carrier bag, with the top and bottom cut off to form a short tube
- Piece of corrugated card, same width as box and 1½ times as long (corrugations should run lengthways if possible)
- Piece of paper 10 x 10cm
- Large rubber band
- Masking or sticky tape
- Compass
- Pencil
- Ruler
- Scissors

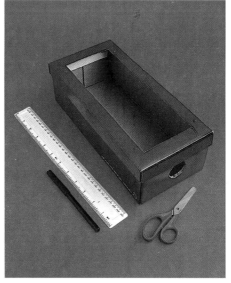

1 Mark all the way round the lid, 2.5cm in from the edge. Cut out the centre. Cut a 2.5cm-diameter hole in the centre of one end of the box.

2 Use tape to stick one edge of the plastic-bag tube along the edge of the lid. Stick down both long sides and one short side. Make sure it is well stuck down, especially at the corners.

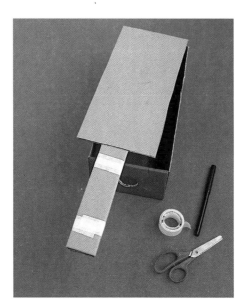

3 Put the box on the corrugated card and draw a line across it. Measure a third in from each long side, cut and fold the sides in to make a handle. Stick the handle together with tape.

When bee keepers open up a beehive, they use small bellows to puff smoke around the bees. This makes the bees sleepy and less likely to sting.

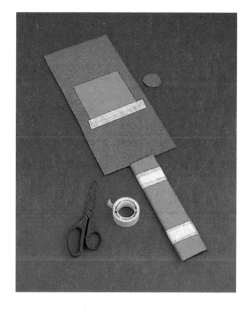

4 Mark the middle of the corrugated card, and draw a circle that has a diameter of about 2.5cm. Cut it out to make a round hole. Tape the piece of paper over the hole, with the tape on the edge nearest to the handle.

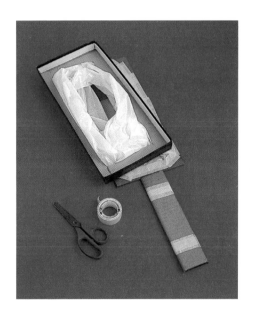

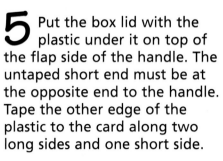

5 Put the box lid with the plastic under it on top of the flap side of the handle. The untaped short end must be at the opposite end to the handle. Tape the other edge of the plastic to the card along two long sides and one short side.

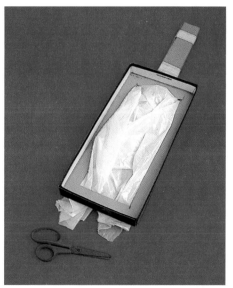

6 Cut the bag in two at the short end, where it has not been stuck down. Pleat each side and cut off the leftover plastic so that it is the same length as the box lid.

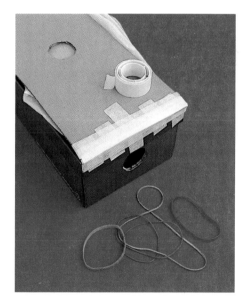

7 Turn it all over and tape across the short edge to join the handle to the box lid. Use several pieces of tape to make a strong, airtight hinge. Put the lid on the box and hold it in place with a rubber band.

FASCINATOR

YOU WILL NEED

- Strong box such as a shoe box
- Three pieces of wooden dowel, approx 5mm diameter: two pieces approx 7cm longer than width of box; one piece 3cm long
- Two discs of corrugated card, 16cm diameter
- Two disks of corrugated card, 14cm diameter
- One disc of corrugated card, 8cm diameter
- One disc of thin card, approx 25cm diameter
- Cotton reel
- Four 1cm pieces of PVC tubing approx 5mm diameter, cut vertically down one side
- Approx 20 small rubber bands
- PVA glue
- Scissors
- Ruler
- Paints or felt-tip pens

This Fascinator is fun to make and fascinating to watch. Turn the handle slowly and the top disc will turn much faster. Once you have made it, you can test optical effects and illusions.

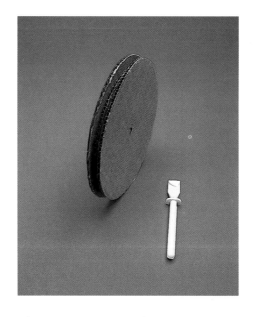

1 Make a pulley wheel from the cardboard discs. Glue together the 14cm discs, then glue the 16cm discs on either side. Let the glue dry. Make a 4mm hole in the centre.

2 On each side of the box, make a hole just big enough to fit the dowel so it can turn freely. The holes must be 10cm from one end, and exactly opposite each other.

When you ride a bicycle, the push made by pedalling is carried by the chain to the cogs on the back wheel. This pushes the bicycle along.

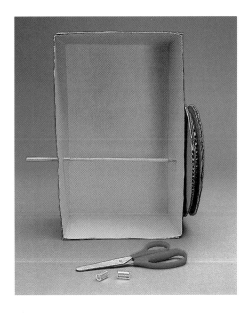

3 Push a long piece of dowel through the holes. Glue the pulley wheel on one end. Put two pieces of PVC tube around the dowel inside the box so that it cannot move from side to side.

4 Make two 4mm holes in the 8cm card disc: one in the centre and another near the edge. Glue the small piece of dowel in the outer hole, then glue the disc on the other end of the long dowel. Let the glue dry.

5 Draw or paint a pattern on the thin card disc. Glue the cotton reel to the other side. Let the glue dry and make a hole in the centre of the disc.

NOW TRY THIS

Design large discs with different patterns and clip them on with paper clips. Try multi-coloured paper discs and see how they blend. What happens when you use red and yellow on one disc?

6 Make two opposite holes at the other end of the box, about 3cm from the end. Push the dowel through the card and cotton reel, and the holes in the box. Put pieces of PVC tube on the dowel at each end to hold it in place.

7 Tie together small rubber bands to make a drive belt around both pulley wheels. Tie the ends together. Turn the handle to check that the machine works. Make the belt longer or shorter if necessary.

GLOSSARY

axle	A wood or metal rod on which a wheel turns.
cable	A strong metal wire, used for electricity or to pull heavy loads.
catapult	A machine worked with levers and ropes to throw objects. Big catapults were used during wars to throw fire balls and rocks.
cog	A wheel that has teeth sticking out from it, to turn another wheel.
cradle	A framework that is specially shaped to hold an object.
crank	Part of an axle or shaft that is bent at right angles to change a circular movement to a backwards and forwards movement.
diagonal	A straight line joining two opposite corners of a square or an oblong.
diameter	The distance across the centre of a circle, from one side to the other.
drive belt	A belt that goes round two different wheels, making them both move.
friction	The force that slows movement when one thing rubs against another.
gravity	The pull of the earth that makes things fall to the ground when they are dropped.
hinge	A joint that moves, allowing objects such as doors and widows to open and close.
lever	A bar that does not bend, which can move something by pushing or pulling.
mechanism	Part of a machine.
paddle	Something that moves or is moved by water.
pivot	A point that joins a lever to another lever, or to a base that does not move.
pulley	A special wheel around which a rope is pulled to raise a weight or move an object.
robot	A machine that works like a person.
rhythm	A regular pattern of sounds, such as the sound of a horse's hooves when it is galloping.
shaft	A straight pole, like an axle, that turns round and carries energy via cogs or belts.
springs	Curved or bent pieces of metal. A coiled spring stores energy.
template	A shape used to mark and cut out a number of the same shapes.
tension	When something has been stretched or twisted, such as a rubber band, or a spring.
vane	Something that is moved by air or water.

BOOKS TO READ

Eyewitness Guides: Invention by Lionel Bender, Dorling Kindersley, 1991

Eyewitness Science Guides: How Things Work by Neil Ardley, Dorling Kindersley, 1995

Great Victorians: Brunel and the Victorian Engineers by Nigel Smith, Wayland, 1997

The Inventor Through History by Pete Lafferty, Wayland, 1993

Machine Technology series, Wayland, 1994–95

Norman Invaders and Settlers by Tony Triggs, Wayland, 1992

Starting Technology: Machines by John Williams, Wayland, 1993

Technology in the Time of Ancient Rome by Robert Snedden, Wayland, 1997

Traditions Around the World: Musical Instruments by Louise Tythacott, Wayland, 1995

The Way Things Work by David Macaulay, Dorling Kindersley, 1988

Windmills and How They Work, by Althea and Edward Parker, A&C Black, 1992

TEACHERS' NOTES

In presenting these projects, the authors have been very aware of the need to keep a balance between clear instructions and encouraging children to develop their own solutions.

An understanding of how simple mechanisms work, and how they are still used, is important. In making these machines children can have control over energy and movement. Making models can be very frustrating as ideas often outstrip practical skills at this age, but with acceptance of the possibility of 'technical collapse', and encouragement to explore and try new ways, children will soon enjoy the discoveries that are possible and will understand the processes involved in development.

Mechanisms are often so simple that they go unnoticed: such as a clothes peg (lever) or ball-point pen (spring/stored energy). As children become aware of the main categories – levers, wheels, pulleys, and gears – together a class can build up extensive lists.

Teachers have always used recycled materials, especially for art and craft activities. Although purpose-made components are available, all these machines have been built with scrap materials with the exception of a few items.

Waving Arms It is possible to build up long, complex systems of linked levers. It is also a good exercise to look at a machine or picture of a machine and to analyze the sequence of movements as many are directly related to levers – a wheel can be considered as a lever rotated through 360 degrees. This project has been made and used very successfully by people with special needs.

Mysterious Rollers This simple toy is related to many practical applications we take for granted in modern life: escalators, audio tape and video cassettes, cinema films, shop cash tills, television newsreaders' autocues, car safety belts, printing presses and conveyor belts.

Flying Messenger A chance to experiment as to which way to wind the propeller for sending the messenger in a particular direction. Have plenty of elastic bands ready as tolerance (which in itself can be tested) is strained. Changes to the component sizes will bring about some interesting results.

Weigh-Your-Savings Bank This machine allows for the exploration of calibration and suspension. Calibrated scales can be seen but the mechanism is often hidden. The making can be linked to projects on transport (public weigh bridges/lorry loading), cooking/healthy eating and shopping.

Drum Machine An electric motor could easily be rigged to turn this type of mechanism, or several linked versions. It could be adapted by fitting the crankshaft inside a box with wires instead of threads, to move figures on the top or sides of the box.

Mouse-a-pult Gone are the days when children used the same leverage to catapult ink blobs about the classroom, but many such examples of the use of the lever can be noted. For less able bodied children these mechanisms enable extension of movement and energy. The links to historical projects in building techniques and warfare are also relevant.

Mini Spreader This is a chance to work at a smaller scale. Children might like to list similar mechanisms which kitchen tools use, and explore tool boxes for examples of springs, wheels and levers etc. It is important to use the corrugations in the plastic in the directions shown in the photographs, both for ease of bending, where necessary and for strength.

Bubble Machine This could lead to a discussion on the properties of different materials and the reasons for choosing them.

Cookie Crusher Pulley wheels are often thought of as lifting devices; they can also be lowering and dropping systems. Many of the mechanical linkages in this book have counterparts working in the opposite direction, with energy intake and result reversed: eg, windmill to fan, crankshaft and handle to cycle pedals and wheel.

Twirler The axle could have two cogwheels working two horizontal wheels in opposite directions. Also, this mechanism could be linked to an exploration of methods of dividing circles by measuring angles and by drawing arcs, etc. Templates could be made for cogwheels of different sizes and with varying numbers and lengths of teeth.

Bellows It may be necessary to tape all round the lid to prevent air escaping. Early vacuum cleaners were made with two bellows, worked by each foot in turn, with valves set the other way to suck rather than blow. It might be possible to construct a working model.

Fascinator This is a very simple gear system. Experiment with different sizes and ratios of pulley wheels and compare them with bicycle systems. Two or more drive wheels could be joined, with several drive belts turning separate pulley wheels at different speeds.

INDEX

Acknowledgements

The author and publishers wish to thank the following for their kind assistance with this book: models Kitty Clark, Suhyun Haw, Yasmin Mukhida, Toby Roycroft and Ranga Silva. Also Gabriella Casemore, Kevin Jolley, Zul Mukhida, Ruth Raudsepp, Philippa Smith and Gus Ferguson.

For the use of their library photographs, grateful thanks are due to: Chapel Studios p8 (Zul Mukhida), p13 (John Stevens), p24 (Zul Mukhida); e.t.archive p16 (Biblioteque Nationale Paris); Eye Ubiquitous p5 top (P Thompson), p11 (G Redmayne), p14 (F Leather), p27 (P Seheult); Topham Picturepoint p5 bottom.
All other photographs belong to the Wayland Picture Library: p4, p6, p19 (C Fairclough), p20, p22, p28.